The Pond

Y0-FZB-077

words and photographs by Janice Boland

Richard C. Owen Publishers, Inc.
Katonah, New York

The pond is calm.

The pond is still.

A leaf falls.

A duck swims.

A spider spins a web.

A turtle sits in the sun.

The pond is calm.
The pond is still.